D1047709

A MAYAN ASTRONOMER

IN HELL'S KITCHEN

W. W. Norton & Company · New York · London

A

MAYAN

ASTRONOMER

IN

HELL'S

KITCHEN

poems

Martín Espada

Copyright © 2000 by Martín Espada

For information about permission to reproduce selections from this book,
write to Permissions, W. W. Norton & Company, Inc.,
500 Fifth Avenue, New York, NY 10110

The text of this book is composed in Fairfield Light with the display set in Lithos
Composition by JoAnn Shambier
Manufacturing by Courier Westford
Book design by JAM Design

Library of Congress Cataloging-in-Publication Data

Espada, Martín, 1957–
A Mayan astronomer in hell's kitchen : poems / Martín Espada.
    p.   cm.
ISBN 0-393-04888-8
1. Hispanic Americans—Poetry. I. Title.
PS3555.S53 M39 2000
811'.54—dc21   99-052626

W. W. Norton & Company, Inc., 500 Fifth Avenue, New York, N.Y. 10110
www.wwnorton.com

W. W. Norton & Company Ltd., 10 Coptic Street, London WC1A 1PU

1 2 3 4 5 6 7 8 9 0

This book is dedicated to Abe Osheroff

CONTENTS

III

A LIBRARY OF LIONS

ACKNOWLEDGMENTS

Some of these poems have appeared or will appear in the following publications, to whose editors grateful acknowledgment is made:

Americas Review: "Preciosa Like a Last Cup of Coffee," "The Shiny Aluminum of God," "Pegao," "Ode to Your Earrings"
El Andar: "The Rage of Plantation Days"
Black Warrior Review: "Pitching the Potatoes," "What Francisco Luis Espada Learned at Age Five, Standing on the Dock," "For the Jim Crow Mexican Restaurant in Cambridge, Massachusetts Where My Cousin Esteban Was Forbidden to Wait Tables Because He Wears Dreadlocks"
Boston Globe: "Another Nameless Prostitute Says the Man Is Innocent"
Crazy Horse: "I Apologize for Giving You Poison Ivy by Smacking You in the Eye with the Crayfish at the End of My Fishing Line," "Anarchism and the Parking Meter," "A Cigarette's Iris in the Eye of a Candle"
A Gathering of the Tribes: "My Name Is Espada," "The Mexican Cabdriver's Poem for His Wife, Who Has Left Him," "Ornithology at the Caribe Hilton," "Crucifixion in the Plaza de Armas"
Harper's: "For the Jim Crow Mexican Restaurant in Cambridge, Massachusetts Where My Cousin Esteban Was Forbidden to Wait Tables Because He Wears Dreadlocks"
Illuminations: "Prisoner AM-8335 and His Library of Lions"
Index on Censorship: "Another Nameless Prostitute Says the Man Is Innocent," "Prisoner AM-8335 and His Library of Lions"
Long Shot: "The Eleventh Reason"
Luna: "The Ghost in the Trunk of the Car," "The Janitor's Garden"
Mid-American Review: "Genuflection in Right Field"

Peacework: "Another Nameless Prostitute Says the Man Is Innocent"

Ploughshares: "Thanksgiving"

Poetry Flash: "Another Nameless Prostitute Says the Man Is Innocent"

Poetry Review: "The Eleventh Reason"

Power Lines (Tía Chucha Press): "A Cigarette's Iris in the Eye of a Candle"

The Progressive: "Another Nameless Prostitute Says the Man Is Innocent," "My Father As a Guitar"

Southern Humanities Review: "The Death of Carmen Miranda"

Southwest Review: "The River Will Not Testify"

Spud Songs (Helicon Nine Editions): "Pitching the Potatoes"

Tampa Review: "The Governor of Puerto Rico Reveals at His Inaugural That He Is the Reincarnation of Ponce de León"

The Threepenny Review: "A Mayan Astronomer in Hell's Kitchen"

Verse: "Compañero Poet and the Surveillance of Sheep"

The Volunteer: "The Carpenter Swam to Spain"

Yes!: "Prisoner AM-8335 and His Library of Lions"

"Thanksgiving" appeared in *The 1999 Pushcart Prize XXIII: Best of the Small Presses*

"For the Jim Crow Mexican Restaurant in Cambridge, Massachusetts Where My Cousin Esteban Was Forbidden to Wait Tables Because He Wears Dreadlocks" appeared in *The Beacon Best of 1999*

Many thanks to Jack Agüeros, Doug Anderson, Katherine Gilbert-Espada, Frances Goldin, Frank Lima, Roberto Márquez, Robert Meeropol, Bill Newman, Sister Dianna Ortíz, Abe Osheroff, Matthew Rothschild, María Luisa Shaghaghi, Gloria Vando, and Ronald Welburn for their support of this work. This work was supported in part by a grant from The Marion Center, College of Santa Fe, for the project National Millenium Survey.

I

A

TARANTULA

IN

THE

BANANAS

My Name Is Espada

Espada: the word for sword in Spain
wrought by fire and the hammer's chime,
name for the warrior reeling helmut-hooded
through the pandemonium of horses in mud,
or the face dreaming on a sarcophagus,
hands folded across the hilt of stone.

Espada: sword in el Caribe,
rapier tested sharp across the bellies of indios, steel tongue
lapping blood like a mastiff gorged on a runaway slave,
god gleaming brighter than the god nailed to the cross,
forged at the anvil with chains by the millions
tangled and red as the entrails of demons.

Espada: baptizing Taíno or Congolese,
name they stuttered in the barking language
of priests and overseers, slave's finger pressed to the blade
with the pulsing revelation that a Spaniard's throat
could seep blood like a fingertip, sabers for the uprising
smuggled in the hay, slave of the upraised saber
beheaded even as the servants and fieldhands
murmured he is not dead, he rides a white horse at night,
his sword is a torch, the master cannot sleep,
there is a dagger under the pillow.

Espada: cousin to the machete, peasant cutlass
splitting the cane like a peasant's backbone,
cousin to the kitchen knife skinning a plátano.
Swords at rest, the machetero or cook
studied their blisters as if planets
to glimpse the hands of their father the horseman,
map the hands of their mother the serf.

Espada: sword in Puerto Rico, family name of bricklayers
who swore their trowels fell as leaves from iron trees;
teachers who wrote poems in galloping calligraphy;
saintcarvers who whittled a slave's gaze and a conqueror's beard;
shoemaker spitting tuberculosis, madwoman
dangling a lantern to listen for the cough;
gambler in a straw hat inhabited by mathematical angels;
preacher who first heard the savior's voice
bleeding through the plaster of the jailhouse;
dreadlocked sculptor stunned by visions of birds,
sprouting wings from his forehead, earthen wings in the fire.

So the face dreaming on a sarcophagus,
the slave of the saber riding a white horse by night
breathe my name, tell me to taste my name: Espada.

Preciosa Like a Last Cup of Coffee

—for my grandmother, Luisa Roig, 1908–1997
 Carolina, Puerto Rico

Tata says her wheelchair
has been stolen by the nurses.
She hallucinates the ceiling fan
spinning closer, the vertigo
of a plummeting helicopter,
but cannot raise her hands
against the blades. Her legs jerk
with the lightning that splits trees.
She scolds her dead sister,
who studies Tata's face
from a rocking chair by the bed
but does not answer.
The grandchildren are grateful
for the plastic diaper, the absence of bedsores.

Tata's mouth collapses without teeth;
her words are miners blackened in the hole.
Now a word pushes out: *café*.
No coffee for her, or she won't eat,
says the nurse.
Tata craves more than a puddle
in a styrofoam cup:
the coffee farm in Utuado, 1928,
the mountains hoisting a harvest of clouds,
the beans a handful of planets,

the spoon in the cup a silver oar,
and the roosters' bickering choir.

But no coffee today.
Cousin Bernice crawls into the bed,
stretches her body across Tata's body
like a drowsy lover, mouth hovering
before her grandmother's eyes
as she chants the word: Preciosa.

Preciosa like the song,
chorus brimming from a kitchen radio
on West 98th Street after the war,
splashing down the fire escape,
preciosa te llaman.
An island from the sky
or a last cup of coffee.
Tata repeats: *Preciosa.*
The song bathes her tongue.

THE SHINY ALUMINUM OF GOD

—Carolina, Puerto Rico, 1997

After the pilgrimage
to the Office of Cemetery Records,
we pay fifty dollars in cash
for the free municipal burial plot,
the clerk hiding the bills in a manila folder.
El pastor Pentecostal forgets the name of the dead,
points at the ceiling and gazes up
whenever he loudly whispers the syllables
for eternal life, *la vida eterna,*
as if the stain on the tile were the map of heaven.
The mourners are palm trees in the hallelujah wind,
hands raised overhead. Once grandmother Tata's pen
looped the words of the spirits as they spoke to her;
now she grips a borrowed golden crucifix
in the coffin, lid propped open by mistake.
The coffin bumps into a hole of mud
next to the chain-link fence, and then
the family Vélez Espada gathers for dinner.

The pernil is frozen, pork shoulder congealed and raw
like a hunk of Siberian woolly mammoth.
But Angela tells us of the miracle pot
that will roast the meat in an hour
without a cup of water. She sells the pot
to her neighbors too, keeps a tower of boxes

with a picture of the pot resplendent on every box.
The words on her kerchief hail
the shiny aluminum of God: Dios te ama.

The scar carves her husband's forehead
where the doctors scooped the tumor out,
where cancer cells scramble like a fistful of ants.
In a year he will be the next funeral, when the saints
of oncology surrender their weapons. For now
Edwin lives by the finches he snares in the backyard,
wings blundering through the trapdoor of the cage,
sold for five dollars apiece to the neighbors.
He praises God for brain surgery and finches,
leans close and grins about the time
his brother somersaulted out a window
and two swooping angels caught him
by the elbows, inches from the ground.
Only one broken rib, Edwin says,
rubbing his stomach in the slow way
of a man satisfied with his meal.
Angela's brother passes out pamphlets:
God's ambulance found him and his needle
in a condemned building, no shoes
and no heartbeat. Then Edwin says:
God will not let me die.

An hour later,
the pernil is still frozen in the oven.
Angela stares at the sweating pork,
then the boxes of pots unsold in the corner.

A boy cousin taps his fork
and asks if we can eat the finches.
The trap clatters in the backyard,
an angel flapping in the cage.

My Father As a Guitar

The cardiologist prescribed
a new medication
and lectured my father
that he had to stop working.
And my father said: *I can't.*
The landlord won't let me.
The heart pills are dice
in my father's hand,
gambler who needs cash
by the first of the month.

On the night his mother died
in faraway Puerto Rico,
my father lurched upright in bed,
heart hammering
like the fist of a man at the door
with an eviction notice.
Minutes later,
the telephone sputtered
with news of the dead.

Sometimes I dream
my father is a guitar,
with a hole in his chest
where the music throbs
between my fingers.

FOR THE JIM CROW MEXICAN RESTAURANT IN CAMBRIDGE, MASSACHUSETTS WHERE MY COUSIN ESTEBAN WAS FORBIDDEN TO WAIT TABLES BECAUSE HE WEARS DREADLOCKS

I have noticed that the hostess in peasant dress,
the wait staff and the boss
share the complexion of a flour tortilla.
I have spooked the servers at my table
by trilling the word *burrito*.
I am aware of your T-shirt solidarity
with the refugees of the Américas,
since they steam in your kitchen.
I know my cousin Esteban the sculptor
rolled tortillas in your kitchen with the fingertips
of ancestral Puerto Rican cigarmakers.
I understand he wanted to be a waiter,
but you proclaimed his black dreadlocks unclean,
so he hissed in Spanish
and his apron collapsed on the floor.

May La Migra handcuff the wait staff
as suspected illegal aliens from Canada;
may a hundred mice dive from the oven
like diminutive leaping dolphins
during your Board of Health inspection;
may the kitchen workers strike, sitting
with folded hands as enchiladas blacken
and twisters of smoke panic the customers;
may a Zapatista squadron commandeer the refrigerator,
liberating a pillar of tortillas at gunpoint;

may you hallucinate dreadlocks
braided in thick vines around your ankles;
and may the Aztec gods pinned like butterflies
to the menu wait for you in the parking lot
at midnight, demanding that you spell their names.

PEGAO

We Puerto Ricans say
that the hard rice
stuck to the bottom
of the pot
is a delicacy.
We scrape
with the spoon
like kitchen archaeologists.

Maybe it's the cost of rice.
Maybe we see the rice
stuck to the bottom
of the pot
as a metaphor.
Or maybe
we have learned to chew
the ow in pegao.

THE GOVERNOR OF PUERTO RICO
REVEALS AT HIS INAUGURAL THAT HE
IS THE REINCARNATION OF PONCE DE LEÓN

—January 1997

Marching through Florida in 1513,
Juan Ponce de León
smacked a mosquito against his neck
and cursed the fountain of youth.
His tongue was breaded with saliva;
cracks webbed his lips.
Ponce de León squinted at the sky,
remembering San Juan,
where as governor he could drowse
to the mating songs of frogs at dusk,
stroking his goatee
in contemplation of gold mines.
Again he smacked his welted neck
and tottered in his armor,
a tortoise straining to walk like a man.

Flash five centuries. The tongue
of Ponce de León is dust
behind a marble slab
in the cathedral of San Juan.
The elected governor of Puerto Rico
salutes the assembly at his inaugural,
as eight-ounce boxes of spring water
with the governor's picture
circulate throughout the crowd.

On the box, his posture is upright
with hands folded
like the high school principal of a nation.
At the gates of the conquistadores' fortress,
the governor announces
that he is the reincarnation
of Juan Ponce de León,
that he has dipped his smooth hands
in the fountain of youth at last, yes,
that all Puerto Ricans
will live forever
and always have rice and beans
if they drink the spring water
with his picture on the box.
"*¡Brindis!*" someone cries.
The crowd toasts the reincarnation
of the thirsty conquistador,
and everyone drinks the water
but the governor.

ORNITHOLOGY AT THE CARIBE HILTON

—San Juan, Puerto Rico, 1998

The white cockatoo from Australia
twirls tricks with a hostess
in white satin dress
for the applause of conferees
on the buffet line;

the scarlet macaw of Brazil
yammers a joke about piña coladas
on a T-shirt in the window
of the gift shop;

the peacock of India
skitters around the koi pond
chased by children
grabbing for a feather from the tail;

the frostbitten turkey from North Carolina
thaws in the kitchen
for the Thanksgiving dinner
devoured on the patio
overlooking the sea;

a Puerto Rican amateur ornithologist
from Brooklyn
contemplates the whitecaps

and the names of birds
ten centuries before the beach was paved,
puffs unseen smoke rings
as his mouth circumnavigates
the Taíno word for hawk: *guaraguao.*

THE RAGE OF PLANTATION DAYS
—Utuado, Puerto Rico, 1938

Utuado at nightfall,
darkness the ink of an octopus
staining the sky between mountains.
The peasant dance, the rum burning like kerosene
in their throats, dimming their eyes.
Then the shouting over money or a woman,
the kerosene lamp splintered by machete,
machetes gripped in the rage of plantation days.
The patrón sleeping in the darkness of octopus sky.

At an early hour, the procession through the plaza,
the corpse sagging in a canvas hammock
shouldered between poles, bloodstains
dawning on the hills of the body, and a boy
with a broom on the church steps,
who once sobbed when he killed a lizard, watching.

WHAT FRANCISCO LUIS ESPADA LEARNED AT AGE FIVE, STANDING ON THE DOCK

Sometimes

there's a

tarantula

in the

bananas

II

A

MAYAN

ASTRONOMER

IN

HELL'S

KITCHEN

THE MEXICAN CABDRIVER'S POEM FOR HIS WIFE, WHO HAS LEFT HIM

We were sitting in traffic
on the Brooklyn Bridge,
so I asked the poets
in the backseat of my cab
to write a poem for you.

They asked
if you are like the moon
or the trees.

I said no,
she is like the bridge
when there is so much traffic
I have time
to watch the boats
on the river.

A Mayan Astronomer in Hell's Kitchen

—9th Avenue and West 48th Street, New York,
   October 1998

Above the deli in Hell's Kitchen where the fire erupted,
above the firefighters charging with hoses like great serpents,
above the fingerprints of smoke smearing the night,
above the crowd calling his name with tilted faces,
above the fire truck and its ladder reaching for him,

a man leaned elbows on the third-floor fire escape,
bronze skin, black hair in a braid, leather jacket,
with a grin for the firefighters
bellowing at the crowds to *stand back*,
a Mayan astronomer in Hell's Kitchen
watching galaxies spiral in the fingerprints of smoke,
smoking a cigarette.

THE JANITOR'S GARDEN
—for Félix Rodríguez, Aibonito, Puerto Rico, 1997

The office building at 42nd and Lexington
sat awaiting the night janitor
like an executive anticipating a shoeshine:
sixty floors mopped and waxed every night,
five nights a week, fifty weeks a year,
for forty-five years: 675,000 floors gleaming.
The ammonia streamed its clear poison
in a cascade, as if from the temple of Ammon
in faraway Egypt, where ammonia began.

He inhaled the burning breath of ammonia
for half a century, and did not die.
He polished the floors for the polished shoes
of industrialists while they slept,
yet did not sleep with rum or wake in sweat.
He stacked the toilet paper of lawyers after midnight
as they stacked contracts and wills,
and did not quiver with desire for their paper.
The janitor kept his garden every night.

When the elevator doors opened
and his mop slid across the floor,
on that glistening spot an orange tree
would sprout, roots fingering through the tile.
A swipe of the mop

and another orange tree scraped the ceiling
with its unfolding fan of branches,
then again till the hallway
was an orange grove in bloom, brilliant
with the trees of China, as people say in Puerto Rico.
The scent of oranges banished ammonia,
and the cleaning crew dripped pulp and juice
to their elbows. Not one sneezed or coughed
in Manhattan slush, walking home after night shift.

On some mornings, a secretary would report
that the floors had been waxed with orange juice,
an errand boy might find peels floating
in all the toilets, or the day janitor discover
an orange in a paper bag scrawled with his name.
The lawyers snorted, blamed the menstrual cycle
or the imagination of colored people, then went to lunch.

Today Félix keeps his garden
in the hills of Aibonito. He is bald as an orange.
Without the ceiling pressing down
the trees become celestial jugglers
levitating orange planets. I climb to the roof
and soak my beard with luminous fruit
as he glances up from the garden,
leaning on his mop.

THE DEATH OF CARMEN MIRANDA

Dying on television,
on the Jimmy Durante Show,
spinning another samba for the tourists
when she staggered beneath the banana headdress
and dropped to one knee.
The audience began to giggle
at the wobbly pyramid of bananas,
but the comedian with the fat nose and the fedora
growled "Stop the music!" and lifted her up.
"I cannot find my breath," Carmen said,
fingers fanning across her chest.
The mouth of the camera opened
to chuckle at her accent, but then
widened into an astonished *"Oh."*

Later that night, at the mansion,
her maid found Carmen sleeping without breath,
could not unlock the mirror from her fingers.
The hair no one saw on television was unpinned,
grown long beneath the banana headdress,
bleached yellow like the bananas.

THE COMMUNITY COLLEGE REVISES ITS CURRICULUM IN RESPONSE TO CHANGING DEMOGRAPHICS

SPA 100 Conversational Spanish
2 credits

The course
is especially concerned
with giving police
the ability
to express themselves
tersely
in matters of interest
to them

THANKSGIVING

This was the first Thanksgiving with my wife's family,
sitting at the stained pine table in the dining room.
The wood stove coughed during her mother's prayer:
Amen and the gravy boat bobbing over fresh linen.
Her father stared into the mashed potatoes
and saw a white battleship floating in the gravy.
Still staring at the mashed potatoes, he began a soliloquy
about the new Navy missiles fired across miles of ocean,
how they could jump into the smokestack of a battleship.
"Now in Korea," he said, "I was a gunner and the people there
ate kimch'i, and it really stinks." Mother complained that no one
was eating the creamed onions. *"Eat, Daddy."* The creamed onions
look like eyeballs, I thought, and then said, "I wish I had missiles
like that." Daddy laughed a 1950s horror-movie mad-scientist laugh,
and told me he didn't have a missile, but he had his own cannon.
"Daddy, eat the candied yams," Mother hissed, as if he were
a liquored CIA spy telling secrets about military hardware
to some Puerto Rican janitor he met in a bar. "I'm a toolmaker.
I made the cannon myself," he announced, and left the table.
"Daddy's family has been here in the Connecticut Valley since 1680,"
Mother said. "There were Indians here once, but they left."
When I started dating her daughter, Mother called me a half-Black,
but now she spooned candied yams on my plate. I nibbled
at the candied yams. I remembered my own Thanksgivings
in the Bronx, turkey with arroz y habichuelas and plátanos,

and countless cousins swaying to bugalú on the record player
or roaring at my grandmother's Spanish punch lines in the kitchen,
the glowing of her cigarette like a firefly lost in the city. For years
I thought everyone ate rice and beans with turkey at Thanksgiving.
Daddy returned to the table with a cannon, steering the black
steel barrel. "Does that cannon go boom?" I asked. "I fire it
in the backyard at the tombstones," he said. "That cemetery bought
up all our farmland during the Depression. Now we only have
the house." He stared and said nothing, then glanced up suddenly,
like a ghost had tickled his ear. "Want to see me fire it?" he grinned.
"Daddy, fire the cannon after dessert," Mother said. "If I fire
the cannon, I have to take out the cannonballs first," he told me.
He tilted the cannon downward, and cannonballs dropped
from the barrel, thudding on the floor and rolling across
the brown braided rug. Grandmother praised the turkey's thighs,
said she would bring leftovers home to feed her Congo Gray parrot.
I walked with Daddy to the backyard, past the bullet holes
in the door and his pickup truck with the Confederate license plate.
He swiveled the cannon around to face the tombstones
on the other side of the backyard fence. "This way, if I hit anybody,
they're already dead," he declared. He stuffed half a charge
of gunpowder into the cannon, and lit the fuse. From the dining room,
Mother yelled, *"Daddy, no!"* Then the battlefield rumbled
under my feet. My head thundered. Smoke drifted over
the tombstones. Daddy laughed. And I thought: When the first
drunken Pilgrim dragged out the cannon at the first Thanksgiving—
that's when the Indians left.

PITCHING THE POTATOES

My father was a semipro pitcher in the city,
with a curveball that swooped
like a seagull feeding at the dump.
One day he slipped on infield grass
and heard his shoulder crunch.
Still, pitching to me years later,
his curveball would sometimes tease
my clutching mitt, and thump my chest.

My younger brother wouldn't eat the mashed potatoes.
I smirked, belly pregnant with tubers,
a toad full of dragonflies. My brother's potatoes
would soon slide down my amphibian gullet.

But my father's jaw was quivering: "You won't eat, hah?"
Then the plate of mashed potatoes
sailed over my brother's bristling crewcut head,
splattered and pasted itself to the wall,
a white oval staring at us from the white plaster
like minimalist art.

My toad eyes strained alertly.
That wasn't the curveball.
My mother bowed her head, another silent prayer,
though I think God was listening to thunderstorms in the Amazon.

The plate began to slide down the wall.
Later, my mother sponged away the mashed potatoes.
I wanted to lick the sponge.

My mother still prays today; she is patient with God.
My brother is a vegetarian.
My father says the Giants have no pitching.
In my sleep, I duck beneath a plate of mashed potatoes
orbiting my head, like a fake flying saucer
suspended by wire
in a snapshot from thirty years ago.

GENUFLECTION IN RIGHT FIELD

We played hardball
in a triangle of grass by the highway ramp.
The outfield was dangerous:
the ball hopping off the roof of a car,
driver leaning big-fisted from the window
like a furious newscaster
bursting through the television screen.
Once a boy we knew
from the neighborhood
circled us, whirling a chain overhead.
We left him sobbing in the grass
after the chain slapped his knees.

One afternoon, we found a pit in right field.
A dog curled dead at the bottom,
fur charred in clumps, a stake jammed
in the split eye socket. We told each other
we had seen this before: the human corpse
bleeding through white plastic garbage bags
and dumped on the hill not far away.
We swore we heard that body moan,
and named the place Dead Man's Hill,
police tape holding us back
like the red velvet rope of a museum.

But the dog was here. We took our positions
with the ceremonial pounding of fist into glove.
The smart hitters poked the ball into right field,
knowing that not one of us could chase it
without pausing at the grave
to glimpse the snarl of a putrified snout,
a fumbling genuflection, the wobbly throw,
the hooting of obscenities from the infield.

The Ghost in the Trunk of the Car

I had a new apartment
for ninety dollars a month.
Roberta brought me a mattress
from the dump at the trailer park,
helped me sponge the dripping bag
of potatoes under the sink
and the handprints
like Neanderthal cave paintings
off the living room wall.

Beers later, she handed me
the snapshot of her boyfriend Buddy.
She missed his drooping convict mouth,
his fingers yellow from years of jailhouse nicotine.
They escaped together
from the mental hospital brooding in the woods
like an insomniac with many eyes.
Every day for a month, when a guard unlocked the gate,
Roberta would sit under the same pine tree
with a bag of knitting, unreeling yards of red and blue
as Buddy's head sank into her lap.
One day, she called a taxi first;
instead of knitting in the bag, their thin clothes.
They worked at a stable somewhere in Wyoming,
miles of empty blacktop

from the hospital with many eyes.
Buddy was shoveling the stalls
when the cops encircled him,
watching him quietly as the horses.

Once I borrowed her green Dodge Dart.
"There's something I should tell you
about the car," Roberta said,
searching her purse for the keys.
"It was used in a murder.
There was a body in the trunk."
Roberta guaranteed that Buddy
was not the killer, then showed me
which key opened the gas cap.

All night I saw the body in the trunk.
I longed to press my ear against the trunk
and listen for the banging of muffled fists.
I wanted to sniff the keyhole of the trunk
like a police dog gathering evidence.
I dreamed about the trunk popping open,
a corpse in whiteface sitting up
and jabbering about his privacy.

I was still pondering the trunk
when I backed the car through an alley,
swung the nose of the green Dodge Dart
into a telephone pole
and crunched it crooked as Buddy's nose

in the snapshot taped
to the rearview mirror.

The ghost in the trunk of the car
muttered about his luck,
rolled over, and went back to sleep.

THE MAN WHO OWNS THE DUMPSTER OWNS THE BOOKS

—Cambridge, Massachusetts

I saw a procession on Church Street,
shoulders hefting crates that brimmed with books.
Here in Harvard Square, I thought,
this must be a train of pilgrims
off to some festival at the temple of the word,
a carnival of poets twirling red scarves
or a conference on scatology.

Then each crate shook into a dumpster:
Books flapped, plummeting,
a collision of flightless birds soon extinct.
The procession of dumpster monks weaved
back to the bookstore where a sign
with letters brooding like a poet's eyebrows
announced: *Out of Business*.

"Why are you throwing out the books?"
I asked the man at the counter.
"Couldn't sell them," he replied,
eyeglasses pinched together by tape,
sweater missing two buttons.
We watched as philosophy professors,
students from the law school,
immigrant cab drivers
and novelists without publishers

crawled into the dumpster,
scooping books and sniffing the air
like looters wary of sirens.

"The man who owns the dumpster owns the books,"
said the man at the counter, phoning the police.
I asked to use the phone, called the librarian
at the city jail, and whispered:
"Tell your class to write an apology poem
and drive down here now."

Soon a cop guarded the dumpster
against the book-looters,
glancing at his shiny black shoes after every plea.
Meanwhile, at a campus art museum of my imagination,
thieves passed oil paintings from the Renaissance
through a hole in the ceiling.

The truck to tow away the dumpster
lumbered onto Church Street as I left.
The jailhouse librarian waited in his car
behind a rusted drawbridge.
His inmate students apologized in rhyme.
Their school was called Saint Dismas,
for the thief who was saved at the crucifixion,
and the sign on their refrigerator read: *Thou Shalt Not Steal*.

ODE TO YOUR EARRINGS
—for Katherine

There are parrots of the Amazon peeking from your hair.

On your earlobes twin Taíno goddesses of the river
squat, their eyes in slits, and dream
the cloud of underwater birth.
Here two Zuni dancers bend and breathe
into their flutes;
here float the smallest leaves and pinecones
from Thoreau's sanctuary,
woven on the loom of trees.

Your ears must be the shoreline
of an ocean after the hurricane:
the seahorses of Thailand curl their tails,
brushing your neck;
purple wooden fish flit past,
hiding in the shade of your hand
when you stroke your hair;
the fish of clay hide, too, shunned by the others
because their skin is fired earth;
and the silver dolphins somersault
in an arc forged like a sickle.

Gold coins pressed from fingers to ears
in the mirror bring a flash

of fingers shoveling the mines.
You keep the plastic pearl earrings
of my grandmother so your hands will know
the Bronx, coffee in a sock on the stove,
the sewing machine's stinger.

One earring lost: dried violets widowed,
turquoise stone in a shield left to tarnish,
peacock feathers painted blue with yellow eyes
still searching for a mate, solitary amethyst,
diminutive lion of wood hunting alone.

But in your ears
you hear the Zuni flute, the branches
shuttling their loom, the dolphin chatter,
a prayer at the wake of the gold miner.
You nod at my grandmother's tranquilidad
de Puerto Rico, serene as the sewing machine at rest.
The goddesses and birds chant in your hair
the recipe for the creation of planets.

Then you stir me from my sleep,
and at night you tell me what you hear.

I Apologize for Giving You Poison Ivy by Smacking You in the Eye with the Crayfish at the End of My Fishing Line

—for Katherine

I apologize for not knowing how to fish.
In Brooklyn all the fish are dead,
from the goldfish spinning in the toilet bowl
to the bluefish on ice at the market
with eyes like Republicans campaigning for Congress.
Once my brother and I went fishing on a lake.
We argued about who was rowing wrong
for half an hour, until we discovered
that the boat was still chained to the dock.

I apologize for not knowing poison ivy.
In my neighborhood everything was poisoned,
the silver clouded water from the tap
and the rainbow gasoline puddle at the curb.
The bricklayer inside my body
stacked the bricks of pollution row by row, so now
if I eat fresh vegetables I might have a stroke.
But I can sit for hours in a patch of poison ivy
without a single welt, head bobbing
as Joe Cuba yells *bang-bang* in the headphones.

(I apologize to the crayfish impaled on my hook.
I am a killer with fogged vision and a tremor in my hands.
I was told that if I went fishing I would relax
and my hands would stop shaking, so the crayfish,
cockroach of the lake, became the panicky bait.
In Puerto Rico the cockroaches

are bigger than this crayfish and they fly,
and no one uses them for bait.)

I apologize for tangling my fishing line in the poison ivy
and whipping it free at the moment
you approached me with an offering of lemonade.
I apologize for the hooked crayfish, oiled with poison ivy,
that flew over my shoulder like a cockroach with wings
and smacked you in the eye.

I apologize for the way your eye ballooned
so you resembled a middleweight
the referee would rescue against the ropes.
I apologize for the splotches that erupted
in scarlet fireworks across your face.
I apologize for the emergency room.
I apologize for the bills from the hospital
that pile like a snowdrift against the mailbox;
when the credit agency calls,
I tell the man that I have a gun
and I know where he works.

I have decided on my penance.
I will return to the lake at midnight
in my swim trunks, and stand there
with arms spread stiff
like a scarecrow beckoning mosquitos,
and as they milk my veins
I will shout this poem repeatedly
til sunrise, or until the police
club me with their flashlights.

If you don't,
my father said,
you better learn
to eat soup
through a straw,
'cause I'm gonna
break your jaw

III

A

LIBRARY

OF

LIONS

CRUCIFIXION IN THE PLAZA DE ARMAS

—Viejo San Juan, Puerto Rico, 1998

By the fountain of statues in the plaza,
next to a sign where fractured letters protest torture by police,
a Black man stands shirtless and pinned to a cross arms wide
like the wingspan of a slave executed for trying to fly,
as high school students bounce to the tambourine
in plena improvisation and tourists from the trolley
crowd into the shop across the street
to search for carvings dark and sleek
as his scarred body, to hunt down their own Black Christ.

COMPAÑERO POET AND THE SURVEILLANCE OF SHEEP

—for Andrew Salkey, 1928–1995
  Amherst, Massachusetts

Your redbrick house is surrounded by sheep.
They pucker their snouts against the wire fence
and watch for you to slide the window open.
They refuse to believe your coffin has flown
like baggage to England.

Now a college bureaucrat sleeps in your house.
The sheep copulate for the college farm program.
Years ago, we noticed the surveillance of sheep,
loudly said they must be FBI. One day,
an agent will sneeze, his nose clogged
with hay and wool, another shorn with clippers
as he wails about his secret work.
The sheep have never read you, but reports
of your subversion nip their ears, relentless as mites.

Poet, you saw Chile from the window of that house:
the perspiration glimmering in the pouches
beneath the eyes of a weary torturer;
the last note trembling on the E string of a guitar
stripped from the hands of an executed singer;
yet also saw the dark grain in the photographs
of the disappeared, the placard aloft in the plaza;

saw that smoke from the charred books and rooftops
always evaporates in a sky ancient with human fumes.

Teacher, you saw Jamaica from the doorway of that house:
the blood under the right thumbnail of your ancestor
cutting the cane for English tea, Jamaican rum;
the scabbed roads of bullwhip across the ribs,
the head on a pike stabbed in the left ear by crows;
yet also saw the musket blast of the Maroon,
rebel slave stuffing powder and lead into the barrel
as redcoated soldiers bled with astonished eyebrows;
saw maternal cheekbones in the mango fattened
and dropped from the tree, envisioned adolescence
in a wooden fishing boat cradled by the flash of the Caribbean Sea.

Diabetes was your chupacabras, the bloodsucker.
Feet amputated, you hopped without toes.
Your fingers twined around the crook of your cane,
the hands consoling each other
for the loss of their brother feet.
Still, you cackled as I ate too many roasted potatoes
from your table. You wrote an ode to orange chicken;
forbidden ginger ice cream, you tasted the words,
sharp and cold.

The sheep cannot believe the accounts of your death, the ambulance
stumbling too late across craters on the road to the hospital.
The sheep wait for the moment to stampede your library,

chew your books, peer through your window and door.
But because of you, poet, teacher, the sheep must watch me
and everyone who ever gazed at the monument of your bookshelves
or prayed for the nova in your poems to flood the mountains.
The sheep are staring yet.

Your beard still sprouts from my jaw. Because of you,
Chile is a bird pressed flat in my book, Jamaica
a brown hand gathering stones on the beach
for snapping at the noses of gargantuan conquerors.
For you, I savor the burst of air
in the word *compañero*.

A CIGARETTE'S IRIS IN THE EYE OF A CANDLE

—for Sister Dianna Ortíz
   Washington, D.C., April 1996

The White House gleams at nightfall,
a kingdom after death where pillars and fountains
wrap themselves in robes of illumination.
Light bathes in water; water basks in light.

There is a vigil across the street:
Sister Dianna in a sleeping bag,
back swarming with a hundred cigarette burns,
one ember screwed into her skin
for every upside down question mark
dangled by the inquisitors of Guatemala.
None of them saw the candle's iris
in the smoldering eye of a cigarette,
yet tonight candles encircle her,
flames like blurred hummingbirds
around her face, cheekbones
the cliffs of a hunger strike.
A cardboard sign at her feet says:
Who is Alejandro?

The torturers called him Alejandro, boss,
wiped their hands to greet him.
After the cigarettes, they burned her body
with phallic torches, invited him to join
the interrogation of the ripped orifice,

lubricated with blood.
Instead he listened to the cries
like a doctor measuring the breath. Later
she heard him curse in midwestern wheat-field English;
without the blindfold, she saw an Americano, white as ash.
She leapt from his car on the way to the Embassy,
refusing the ash smeared across her skin.

Sister Ortíz simulated the kidnapping,
violated the Eighth Commandment
against false witness, said the U.S. Ambassador.
A sadomasochistic lesbian nun,
said a State Department official.
A case of delicate nerves,
said the Guatemalan Minister of Defense.
The First Lady sat on a couch with her
beneath a constellation of cameras,
careful as a hostess with a wine-befuddled guest.
At the press conference a chorus of spies and bureaucrats
crooned in soprano: There is no Alejandro, no Americano.
In Guatemala, the pit where they dangled her
still writhes with rats and dying fingers,
the cordillera of skulls swells and ripples across the map.

Now Sister Dianna keeps vigil on Pennsylvania Avenue,
sheltered from the drizzle of ambassadors
by a cardboard sign, the vowels in *Alejandro*
becoming the eyes and mouths of the words
she once taught in the Mayan highlands.
The silence in her mouth is the bread she will not eat,

her eyes contemplating the cigarette's iris in the eye of a candle.
The White House is a burnished castle in the distance
where fountains thunder, but no one drinks,
where the word *torture* has been abolished.
From a high window someone peers,
a servant or the head of state, and curses in English.

ANARCHISM AND THE PARKING METER

—San Francisco, California, 1986

As I was about
to put a quarter
in the parking meter,
a man walking by
stopped, whirled,
fired three karate kicks
decapitating the meter,
and stretched out
his hand
for the quarter

THE CARPENTER SWAM TO SPAIN

—for Abe Osheroff
and the Veterans of the Abraham Lincoln Brigade

The ship hushed the waves to sleep at midnight:
Ciudad de Barcelona, Ciudad de Barcelona.

In the name of the aristocrat strolling through his garden
Franco's tanks crawled like a plague of smoldering beetles;
in the name of the bishop and his cathedrals
the firing squads sang a stuttering mass with smoke in their throats;
in the name of the exiled king and blueshirts on the march
bombers with swastika fins sowed an inferno
in village marketplaces and the ribs of the dead.
At Guernica an ancient woman in black stumbled
across a corpse and clawed her hair;
at Víznar, where the spring bubbles, a poet in white shoes
coughed the bullets' blood onto his white shirt,
gypsy sobbing in the cave of his mouth.

Ciudad de Barcelona: The ship plowed the ocean,
and the ocean was a wheat field thinking of bread.
And the faces at the portholes thinking: Spain.

In España, the carpenters and miners kneeled with rifles
behind a barricade of killed horses,
the peasant boys cradled grenades like pomegranates
to fling against the plague of tanks, the hive of helmets.
Elsewhere across the earth, thousands more laid hammers
in toolboxes, holstered drills, promised letters home,

and crowded onto ships for Spain:
volunteers for the Republic, congregation of berets,
fedoras and fist-salutes for the camera, cigarettes and union songs.
The handle of the hammer became the stock of the rifle.

The ship called *Ciudad de Barcelona* steamed
across the thumping tide, hull bearded with foam,
the body of Spain slumbering on the horizon.

Another carpenter read the newspapers
by the tunnel-light of the subway in Brooklyn.
Abe Osheroff sailed for Spain. Because Franco's mustache
was stiff as a paintbrush with his cousins' blood;
because Hitler's iron maw would be a bulldozer,
heaving a downpour of cadavers into common graves.

The ship of volunteers was *Ciudad de Barcelona*,
Abe the carpenter among them, and for them
the word *Barcelona* tingled like the aftertaste of a kiss.
Two miles from shore, they saw the prop plane hover
as if a spectre from the last war,
the pilot's hand jab untranslated warning.
Then the thud, a heart kicking in spasm,
the breastbone of the ship punctured
by a torpedo from Mussolini's submarine.
In seven minutes, the ship called *Ciudad de Barcelona*
tilted and slid into the gushing sea,
at every porthole a face trapped,
mouth round and silent like the porthole.

Eighty mouths round in the high note of silence.
Schultz, captain of the Brooklyn College swim team,
pinned below deck and drowned,
his champion's breaststroke flailing.
Other hands that could swim burst through the wave-walls
and reached for the hands that could not. The boats
of a fishing village crystallized from the foam,
a fleet of saints with salt glistening in their beards,
blankets and rum on the shore.

Abe swam two miles to Spain,
made trowels of his hands
to cleave the thickening water.
His fingers learned the rifle's trigger
as they knew the hammer's claw.
At Fuentes de Ebro, armageddon
babbled and wailed above the trenches;
when he bled there, an ocean of shipwreck
surged through his body. Today, his white beard
is a garland of clouds and sea-foam,
and he remembers Schultz, the swimmer.

Now, for Abe, I tap these words
like a telegraph operator
with news of survivors:
Ciudad de Barcelona, Ciudad de Barcelona.

Author's Note: The Eleventh Reason

Robert Meeropol is the younger son of Julius and Ethel Rosenberg, who were executed in 1953 on charges of conspiracy to commit espionage in the form of passing atomic secrets to the Soviet Union, despite an international outcry protesting their innocence. As a child, Meeropol heard repeated references to "eleventh-hour appeals" and believed that the Rosenbergs' lawyers needed to present eleven reasons why his parents should be spared. They could only produce ten; this explained his parents' execution.

THE ELEVENTH REASON
—for Robert Meeropol

I am dreaming of a courtroom.
I am the one in a blue suit, necktie crooked,
my face blurry in the sheen of a polished table.
I must be the lawyer.
The judge flutters black robes into the courtroom.
The bailiff calls for all to rise, yanks my elbow
when I do not. The judge speaks to me in baritone.
He folds his hands on the bench, and smiles
like a state trooper contemplating a speeding ticket:
Good morning, counsel.
Give me ten reasons why Julius and Ethel Rosenberg
should not be executed today.

I stare at the judge. The lights above my head
are yellow with the spinning bees of amnesia.
Ten reasons, please, the judge says.

I say: Your honor,
someday an FBI agent will confess
in his hot loud sleep, crying that he killed
the Rosenbergs, the password of spies
was his idea for coached witnesses to recall.
The prosecutor will chatter
about his Jell-O box puzzle of evidence,
snipped with his own scissors, but his hands will sweat
and someone will spray paint his real name

across the prosecutor's tombstone.
The mushroom cloud will bloom over the desert
and a city of gamblers, but no Red spies
will peer through binoculars, and soldiers
without helmets will sprout cancers
like cabbages in the stomach.

What about the Rosenbergs? says the judge.

They will walk with sandwich boards
and picket signs through our drowsy dying visions.
They will whisper their prison letters in voices that linger,
so we turn the knobs on the radio to crackle them away,
but their silence will swarm us, and we will swat the air,
howling that a million flies haunt the spirals of our ears.
Their pale oval faces will drift through the subway,
in crowds at the ballgame, his eyeglasses, her hat.
We will see them embrace in a tangle of handcuffs
and swear that we saw nothing.
We will glimpse the electric chair on television
and shriek Jew, Jew, Jew, and then deny we said it,
as the tentacles of leather straps
remember their skin's topography.
We will hear the common stickball names of their sons
called out from the window of a tenement
and sob without knowing why.
We will be unable to look at a clock that reads 6:19,
because that was the date of their execution
and numbers are hard like teeth.

Those are ten reasons, the judge says.
I need eleven. Give me one more.

My face is stinging. I glance down at the table.
I have no files, no folders,
no yellow legal pads, no notes.
Espionage, electrocution, these are not my areas
of expertise. I am a tenant lawyer.
I am not prepared to discuss
the eleventh reason.
I request a continuance.
I promise a memorandum of law
on the eleventh reason.
The judge says no, and smiles.
Thank you, your honor, I hear myself mumble.

In the hallway, I see you, their son,
waiting on a bench. You are not a boy, as in 1953.
Your beard is gray like the judge's beard.
This courtroom flickered in the moviehouse
of your forehead many years ago.

They wanted eleven reasons, I tell you.
I know that, you say, I've known for forty-five years.
Executioners know that the hands have ten fingers.
So they ask for eleven.

Then all of us are killed, I say.
Not yet, you say, squinting past me
at the bailiff shutting the courtroom doors.
Not yet.

Author's Note: Another Nameless Prostitute Says the Man Is Innocent

Mumia Abu-Jamal is a radical African-American journalist on death row, convicted in the 1981 slaying of a police officer in Philadelphia—under extremely dubious circumstances. There is a movement to win him a new trial.

In April 1997, NPR's *All Things Considered* first commissioned, then refused to air, the following poem, due to its subject matter and political sympathies.

ANOTHER NAMELESS PROSTITUTE
SAYS THE MAN IS INNOCENT

—for Mumia Abu-Jamal
   Philadelphia, Pennsylvania/Camden, New Jersey, April 1997

The board-blinded windows knew what happened;
the pavement sleepers of Philadelphia, groaning
in their ghost-infested sleep, knew what happened;
every Black man blessed
with the gashed eyebrow of nightsticks
knew what happened;
even Walt Whitman knew what happened,
poet a century dead, keeping vigil
from the tomb on the other side of the bridge.

More than fifteen years ago,
the cataract stare of the cruiser's headlights,
the impossible angle of the bullet,
the tributaries and lakes of blood,
Officer Faulkner dead, suspect Mumia shot in the chest,
the witnesses who saw a gunman
running away, his heart and feet thudding.

The nameless prostitutes know,
hunched at the curb, their bare legs chilled.
Their faces squinted to see that night,
rouged with fading bruises. Now the faces fade.
Perhaps an eyewitness putrifies eyes open in a bed of soil,
or floats in the warm gulf stream of her addiction,

or hides from the fanged whispers of the police
in the tomb of Walt Whitman,
where the granite door is open
and fugitive slaves may rest.

Mumia: the Panther beret, the thinking dreadlocks,
dissident words that swarmed the microphone like a hive,
sharing meals with people named Africa,
calling out their names even after the police bombardment
that charred their Black bodies.
So the governor has signed the death warrant.
The executioner's needle would flush the poison
down into Mumia's writing hand
so the fingers curl like a burned spider;
his calm questioning mouth would grow numb,
and everywhere radios sputter to silence, in his memory.

The veiled prostitutes are gone,
gone to the segregated balcony of whores.
But the newspaper reports that another nameless prostitute
says the man is innocent, that she will testify at the next hearing.
Beyond the courthouse, a multitude of witnesses chants, prays,
shouts for his prison to collapse, a shack in a hurricane.

Mumia, if the last nameless prostitute
becomes an unraveling turban of steam,
if the judges' robes become clouds of ink
swirling like octopus deception,
if the shroud becomes your Amish quilt,
if your dreadlocks are snipped during autopsy,

then drift above the ruined RCA factory
that once birthed radios
to the tomb of Walt Whitman,
where the granite door is open
and fugitive slaves may rest.

Prisoner AM-8335 and His Library of Lions

—for Mumia Abu-Jamal
  SCI-Greene, Waynesburg, Pennsylvania
  May 2, 1998

When the guards handcuffed inmates in the shower
and shoved them skidding naked to concrete,
or the blueshirts billyclubbed a prisoner
to wrench the gold from his jaw,
to swirl KKK in his spat blood,
the numbered men pressed their fingertips
against the smooth cool pages of your voice,
that voice of many books,
and together you whispered in the yard
about lawsuits, about the newspapers.

From the battlements
the warden trumpeted a proclamation:
in every cell one box per inmate,
twelve by twelve by fourteen,
for all personal possessions. You say
four blueshirts crowded your death row cell
to wrestle seventeen cartons away,
wrinkled paperbacks in pillars
toppling, history or law collected and studied
like the bones of a fossilized predator,
a library beyond Carnegie's whitest visions of marble.
One guard would fondle a book emblazoned
with the word *Revolutionary,* muttering:
this is what we're supposed to get.

Today, after the hunger strike,
you sit windowed in the visiting room,
prisoner AM-8335: dreadlocks blooming
like an undiscovered plant of the rain forest,
hands coupled in the steel cuffs,
brown skin against the striped prison jumpsuit,
tapestry of the chain gang.

I would rather be beaten, you say,
than this assault on the life of the mind.
You keep Toni Morrison's book in your box with the toothpaste.
You stare through the glass at the towering apparition
of your library, as if climbing marble steps.

And you say:
Giving up a book is like giving up a child,
like parting with your own flesh.
How do you choose between *Beloved*
and *The Wretched of the Earth*.

Your eyes pool.
A single tear is the scarification of your cheekbone,
a warrior's ceremonial gash on death row.
Across the glass a reflection of the guards walking,
small blue men patrolling your forehead.

In the parking lot, I turn again toward the prison,
walls ribboned with jagged silver loops of wire,
and see a great library
with statues of lions at the gate.

THE RIVER WILL NOT TESTIFY

—Connecticut River
  Turners Falls, Massachusetts, 1999

The river's belly swirls shards of bone gnawed by water.
The river is deaf after centuries of pummeling the rocks.
The river thrashes all night with the lightning of lunatic visions.
The river strangles on the dam, hissing at the stone eagles
that watch with stone eyes from the bridge.
Concrete stops the river's tongue at Turners Falls.

The river cannot testify to all the names:
Peskeomskut, gathering place at the falls;
Sokoki, Nipmuck, Pocumtuck, many nations, many hands
that speared the flapping salmon from the rocks,
stitched the strips of white birch into wigwams.
So Reverend Mr. Russell wrote to the Council of War:
They dwell at the Falls a considerable number, yet
most of them old men, women and children. The Lord calls us
to make some trial which may be done against them.

The river cannot testify of May 19, 1676.
The river's face was painted blue at daybreak.
Captain Turner's men, Puritans sniffing with beards
and flintlock muzzles, slipped between the wigwams
ghostly as the smoke from drying fish.
Their muskets lifted up the flaps of bark;
their furious God roared from every musket's mouth.

The sleepers drenched in rivers sun-red like the salmon,
and a wailing rose with the mist from the skin of the river.

The river cannot testify about canoes skidding
over the falls, their ribs in splinters, or swimmers
hammering their skulls against the rocks,
or bullets hammering the rocks and skulls,
or Captain Holyoke's sword lopping the branches
of grandfathers into the water, or Bardwell
counting the corpses vomited by the white cascade.
And Reverend Mr. Mather wrote:
The river swept them away, that ancient river, oh my soul.

The river cannot testify to who began the rumor:
a thousand Indians, someone yelled, a thousand Indians approaching;
so when a few dozen warriors read the smoke from gutted wigwams
and splashed across the river, the conquerors fled,
shrieking at the green demons that whipped their eyes
and snatched their ankles as they stumbled through the forest.

The river cannot testify to say what warrior's musket
shot Captain Turner, the ball of lead thudding
between shoulder blades, flipped from his horse
and dragged off by the water to sink in a halo of blood.
His name christened the falls, the town, the granite monument
that says: *destroyed 300 Indians at this place.*
One day a fisherman would unearth shinbones
of Indians by the falls, seven skeletons
and each one seven feet tall, he declared.

Centuries gone, the fishing boats sucked over the dam,
the tendons of the bridge ripped out in the flood,
the children leaning too far and abducted by the current:
all as withered leaves to the river.
The lumber company fire that smothered the night watchman,
the cotton mill and the needles of brown lung,
the knife factory bricked shut during the Depression:
all mosquito-hum and glimmer of porchlight to the river.
The Horse Thief Detecting Society that never caught a thief,
the German Military Band flourishing trombones,
the Order of Scalpers with fraternity war whoops,
the American Legion dinners beery against communism,
the Indians galloping undefeated onto the high school football field:
all like the glitter of fish to the river.

Centuries from now, at this place,
when chimneys are the shadows of monsters in the river,
when collapsed spires are haunted by crows,
when graves are plowed to harvest the bones
for aphrodisiacs and trinkets,
when the monuments of war have cracked
into hieroglyphics no one can read,
when the rain sizzles with a nameless poison,
when the current drunk on its own dark liquor
storms through the crumbling of the dam,
the river will not testify of Turners Falls,
for the river has swept them away, oh my soul.

arroz y (or con) habichuelas: rice and beans

brindis: a toast

bugalú: Latin music popular in New York during the mid-1960s, combining rhythm and blues with traditional Cuban elements and bilingual (Spanish-English) lyrics

el Caribe: the Caribbean

chupacabras: literally, a goatsucker; a mythical creature, perhaps extraterrestrial or supernatural, said to prey on animals in Puerto Rico

Ciudad de Barcelona: City of Barcelona; refers here to a ship torpedoed by fascist forces during the Spanish Civil War

compañero: good friend; may have connotations of political comradeship

Cuba, Joe: bugalú songwriter and bandleader

Dios te ama: "God loves you"

guaraguao: hawk

indio: Indian

machetero: machete-wielder or canecutter

La Migra: Immigration and Naturalization Service

pastor pentecostal: Pentecostal minister

patrón: landowner or boss

pegao: from "pegado," literally "stuck," referring in particular to the crunchy rice stuck at the bottom of the pot

petnil: roast pork shoulder

plátano: plantain

plena: song and dance form originating with the Black population of Ponce, Puerto Rico

Ponce de León, Juan: best known as the conquistador who, according to legend, searched for the fountain of youth in Florida, Ponce de León was the first Spanish governor of Puerto Rico, and is buried there

preciosa te llaman: "they call you beautiful"; from the chorus of a famous song, "Preciosa," by Rafael Hernández, about Puerto Rico

samba: song and dance form originating with the Black population of Brazil

Taíno: original indigenous inhabitants of Puerto Rico, decimated by the Spanish

tranquilidad: serenity; referring here to peace of mind

la vida eterna: "eternal life"

Zapatista: contemporary revolutionary movement based in Chiapas, México, and named for Emiliano Zapata, rebel leader in the Mexican Revolution of 1910

Martín Espada was born in Brooklyn, New York, in 1957. His fifth book of poetry, *Imagine the Angels of Bread* (W. W. Norton, 1996), won an American Book Award and was a finalist for the National Book Critics Circle Award. Another volume, *Rebellion Is the Circle of a Lover's Hands* (Curbstone, 1990), won both the PEN/Revson Fellowship and the Paterson Poetry Prize. His poems have appeared in *The New York Times Book Review, Harper's, The Nation, The Pushcart Prize XXIII,* and *The Best American Poetry.* He has published a collection of essays, *Zapata's Disciple* (South End Press, 1998), which received an Independent Publisher Book Award, and is also the editor of *El Coro: A Chorus of Latino and Latina Poetry* (University of Massachusetts Press, 1997), recipient of a Myers Outstanding Book Award. A former tenant lawyer, Espada is currently a professor in the Department of English at the University of Massachusetts-Amherst.